SECRETS
SIGNS
SIGNALS
& CODES

SECRETS
SIGNS
SIGNALS
& CODES

by Shari Lewis

Leo Benhke, Consultant
Illustrations by Helen McCarthy
Art Direction by John Brogna

Holt, Rinehart and Winston
New York

Acknowledgment

Kids-Only Club Book Series advisor Dr. A.B. Hurwitz, formerly Peter Pan the Magic Man, the official magician for the City of New York.

Published by Holt, Rinehart and Winston, 383 Madison Avenue, New York, New York 10017. Published simultaneously in Canada by Holt, Rinehart and Winston of Canada, Limited.

Lewis, Shari.
    Secrets, signs, signals & codes.

    (Kids-only club)
    Includes index.
    SUMMARY: Discusses codes, silent signals, invisible writing, and other ways to conceal messages.
    1. Ciphers—Juvenile literature.   2. Cryptography —Juvenile literature.   3. Writing, Invisible— Juvenile literature.   4. Signs and symbols—Juvenile literature. [1. Ciphers.   2. Cryptography. 3. Signs and symbols] I.   McCarthy, Helen. II. Title.
Z103.3.L48   001.54'36   79-3837
ISBN   0–03–049711–6
ISBN   0–03–049716–7 pbk.

Printed in the United States of America
10   9   8   7   6   5   4   3   2   1

DEDICATION

I gratefully dedicate this Kids-Only Club Book
to Lee Schulman. I used to be a Shari-Only
Club member. Thanks to him, I now belong to
a team.

Contents

FOTO
FUN

Shawn

Barker

Georgia

Jimmy

Mally

Twerp

Introduction

Almost everybody likes secrets. They make us feel good. When you have a secret, you have something that nobody else has!

However, different people like to do different things with secrets:

Some like to *keep* them in a private place. If this describes you, you'll like Stash Your Secret Stuff on pages 33–34.

Other folks like to *share* secrets with their closest friends, even when those close friends are not so close. If you love to send special messages across a noisy schoolyard or across a quiet room or even across the country (when you're on vacation on one coast and your pal is at camp on the other coast) Hidden Messages (pages 16–35) and For Your Eyes Only (pages 11–15) will be perfect fun for you.

There are kids and older folk who are happiest when they're able to *figure out* secrets (Garbled Games, pages 76–93) and others who like to be "in" on the secret signals sent by people living and working in unusual ways (Aircraft Landing Signal Officers, page 56, TV stage managers, page 54 and the Mute Alphabet, page 57.

The Kids-Only Club Gang—Georgia, Jimmy, Shawn, Mally, Twerp and Barker—feel that secrets are personal treasures and they're happy to share this treasure chest of secrets with you.

Georgia slips Jimmy a secret message.

1. For Your Eyes Only

In the language of spies, a "cleartext" is any message that is meant to be read exactly as it is written. For example, this sentence is in cleartext.

However, there are some great ways to write a note in cleartext so that it can only be read by the person who is supposed to read it, because only that person is in on a special secret.

SHUFFLED MESSAGE

Here is one of the most clever ways to hide a message that you can imagine!

Shuffle an old discarded deck of cards and then make a list of the cards from the top to the bottom. You can do it much faster if you use abbreviations—like A for ace, K for king, C for clubs, H for hearts, S for spades, D for diamonds, and so on. Your list should look something like this:

AC, 2S, 5H, 7C, 10D, 4H, 8C, 9C, 2D, AH . . .

Give a copy of the list to each friend with whom you may want to exchange secret messages.

To write a message, arrange an old deck of cards so that it is in the same order as your list. With a *pencil*, write your message on the side edges of the deck, writing two lines on each of the four sides, if you have to.

Also, mark a straight line on one corner so that the line goes across the sides of all of the cards. Shuffle the deck three or four times and hand it or send it to your friend.

When your pal is alone, he or she arranges the deck so that it once again matches the list, and then the message can be read. If the words aren't clear, your friend should look for the line on the marked corner and make sure that all of the cards are turned in the right direction.

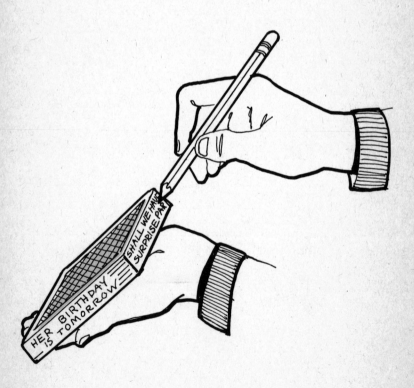

SECRET ON A STICK

The commanders of the Roman and Greek armies generally carried a metal rod decorated with fancy ends. This 12- to 14-inch long stick was called a *scytale*. Only very important generals were allowed to carry these batons.

When one of these military men had to send a secret message to his brother officer, he would wrap a strip of paper around the scytale and then write whatever he had to say *down the length of the rod*. When the paper was unwound, it looked like gibberish instead of an important message. But when the other officer got this silly looking strip of paper, he'd wrap it around his rod, and read the private message.

You can do the same thing and send notes across a room — notes that can't be read by anyone who gets hold of them along the way. Here's how.

Get two matching unsharpened pencils (that way they're sure to be the same length). Give one to your friend and keep the other for yourself.

To send your message, cut a 1-inch strip from the long side of a sheet of typing paper.

Wrap the paper diagonally around the pencil as tightly as possible, leaving less than ¼ inch between each edge on every twist.

Fasten the end of the wrapped paper with the tiniest possible bit of cellophane tape.

Now write the message in a straight line along the side of the pencil, putting only one letter between every two edges, and some letters right *on* the edges.

The message can be two or three lines long, depending on the thickness of the pencil.

Now remove the tape and unwrap the paper. All that anyone can see is a mixture of letters and squiggles scattered along the edges of the strip of paper. Half of a letter will show up in one place, half in another.

When your friend gets the message, he or she can read it by wrapping the paper around a pencil like this:

Hold the strip so that the letters are upright. Start rolling at the bottom and twist as tightly as possible around the pencil. Don't try to read or make sense of the message as it is rolled—just match up the random lines so that they form letters and fit the letters together so that they make words. Then place a tiny piece of tape at the end of the strip, and the secret message will be there for you to see.

If you would like to send a *long* secret message (for example, as a letter) you and your friend will need matching pieces of dowel, or broomsticks.

Instead of tiny strips of paper, try to get hold of some adding machine tape. Then in the same way you can send your Secret On A Stick!

SKIP-A-LETTER

Here's a very easy way to disguise a message. It's easy to read when you know the rule, but it's confusing to the "enemy."

On a sheet of paper, write down your message. Count the letters. Divide the total number by 2. Got the sum? That's the middle of your message. Go back and count off *that* number of letters and draw a line between that and the next letter. (In other words, if your message is 22 letters long, you would draw a line between the 11th and 12th letters.)

On another sheet of paper, write your message in capital letters, *leaving enough space between each letter for another letter.* When you get to the line marking the center of the message, *go back to the beginning of your message and start putting the rest of the letters between the ones you've already written.*

Your friend can read the message by writing down the odd letters (letters 1, 3, 5, etc.) from the beginning to the end. Then your pal goes back to the beginning to write down the even letters, which make up the *second* half of the message.

TIHTITSEMNECSOSRARGEECITSLWYR

If you think someone may be catching on to the method, write the message backwards!

!TSIDRRWASWIKECNAOBSNIEHTT

Answer: This message is written correctly.

15

2. Hidden Messages: Codes and Ciphers

When most people talk about a *code*, what they really mean is a *cipher*. Here's the difference:

A *code* is where a picture, symbol, or word has a specific meaning. In a *cipher*, a letter or symbol is substituted for each individual letter in a message. So if I write the number 3 to mean the word Tuesday, that's a *code*; if I write the numbers 6-3-1-8-2-4-7 to mean Tuesday (one number for each letter), then that is a *cipher*.

That string of numbers is not in *cleartext* (because *cleartext* means that the message is to be read exactly as it's written). Since a number has been substituted for each letter, it is in *ciphertext*.

SHIFTY LETTERS

Here are some really easy ciphers in which you substitute one alphabet for another. In each of these ciphers, *the cleartext alphabet is on top and the cipher is below it.* Look for the letter you want to disguise in the top line, but write the letter *below* it for your secret message.

Forward Shift

The cipher alphabet is moved forward one letter. If you want to say "hello," you'd write "gdkkn," because under the "H" is a "G," and so on. Here's that cipher key:

Cleartext:
A B C D E F G H I J K L M N O P Q R S T U V W X Y Z
Ciphertext:
Z A B C D E F G H I J K L M N O P Q R S T U V W X Y

cipher #1 (for Elliot)

Coded Shift

Let's say the cipher message is "DWHLJKWVKDUS." In this case, the cipher message starts with a "D." The person receiving the message knows that he or she can figure out the secret by placing the letter "D" under the "A" of the real alphabet, and then laying the rest of the alphabet down in sequence after that "D," like this cipher key:

A B C D E F G H I J K L M N O P Q R S T U V W X Y Z
D E F G H I J K L M N O P Q R S T U V W X Y Z A B C

Since the cipher message is

D W H L J K W V K D U S

then the cleartext is

AT EIGHT SHARP.

ORDER, PLEASE!

Here is a simple cipher to use when you want to disguise only certain words in a message. It's also easy to memorize this cipher, since it's just a couple of numbers. That way, you and your pals won't have to write it down and run a risk that someone will find it.

Make a paper strip with the numbers from 1 to 0 (zero will replace 10) in two groups of five each. Mix up the numbers and write them along the bottom edge. It could look like this—

```
6 4 0 2 8     7 1 9 3 5
```

Make one copy for each really good friend.

To write your secret put the first letter of your message under number 1, the second under number 2, and so on. For example, if you wanted to write GO WITH JANE, the ciphertext would look like this—

```
6 4 0 2 8     7 1 9 3 5
```

H I E O A   J G N W T

If your message is more than ten letters long, just move the strip to the right and jot down the next letters in the same way. If your message has fewer than ten letters, finish with letters that clearly don't have anything to do with the message, like K, Q, X and Z.

ACROSS AND DOWN

With this system you can have a different cipher for each day of the week because there are eight different ways to arrange the alphabet.

Make a grid of the alphabet, with five letters across

and five letters down. Since there are 26 letters in our alphabet, you have to put Y and Z together in the last square. Don't worry about this. People decoding your ciphertext will understand which letter to use when they read the message.

On the top and left side of this box of letters, put the numbers from 1 to 5 (they go outside the grid).

	1	2	3	4	5
1	A	B	C	D	E
2	F	G	H	I	J
3	K	L	M	N	O
4	P	Q	R	S	T
5	U	V	W	X	Yz

Draw matching Across and Down Alphabet Grids for your friends.

To make up a cipher message, look for the letter you want, and write the number that's at the top of its column, going across, and then the number of its row, going down. Let's say you want to write

DO IT NOW

Here's the ciphertext: 14–35 24–45 34–35–53.

That's one! Here are seven other ways to arrange your alphabet:

	1	2	3	4	5
1	A	F	K	P	U
2	B	G	L	Q	V
3	C	H	M	R	W
4	D	I	N	S	X
5	E	J	O	T	Yz

	1	2	3	4	5
1	U	V	W	X	Yz
2	P	Q	R	S	T
3	K	L	M	N	O
4	F	G	H	I	J
5	A	B	C	D	E

	1	2	3	4	5
1	E	J	O	T	Yz
2	D	I	N	S	X
3	C	H	M	R	W
4	B	G	L	Q	V
5	A	F	K	P	U

	1	2	3	4	5
1	E	D	C	B	A
2	J	I	H	G	F
3	O	N	M	L	K
4	T	S	R	Q	P
5	Yz	X	W	V	U

	1	2	3	4	5
1	U	P	K	F	A
2	V	Q	L	G	B
3	W	R	M	H	C
4	X	S	N	I	D
5	Yz	T	O	J	E

	1	2	3	4	5
1	Yz	X	W	V	U
2	T	S	R	Q	P
3	O	N	M	L	K
4	J	I	H	G	F
5	E	D	C	B	A

	1	2	3	4	5
1	Yz	T	O	J	E
2	X	S	N	I	D
3	W	R	M	H	C
4	V	Q	L	G	B
5	U	P	K	F	A

SQUARE CIPHER

This is an exciting cipher because even if people find the sheet with your alphabet squares, they probably won't be able to figure out your secret message!

Draw the alphabet in the squares shown. As you can see, Y and Z are not in this cipher. If they are in the cleartext (that is, if Y and Z are in your real message), simply use Y and Z in the cipher message.

To write your message in a secret way, find each letter of the message, then *write down the letter that is in the same position in the square across from it.* For example, if you want the letter C, write O; if you want P, use D. Here is a message and its ciphertext:

Cleartext: HELP, QUICK!

Ciphertext: TQXD EIUOW!

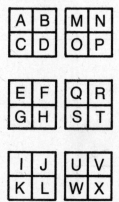

SCRAMBLED STRIPS

In this cipher you don't use an alphabet, you use the message itself.

Write your message in lines of five letters each, and if you come out with less than a full line at the end, fill in the remaining spaces with extra letters. So if your secret message is "Use this cipher today," the letters would look like this—

```
U S E T H
I S C I P
H E R T O
D A Y X J
```

Now you need a keyword. It has to have five letters, all different. You might use the name of the person who is receiving the cipher, or your own name, or the name of an object; *anything* can be used as long as both you and the person getting the message know it.

Write this keyword above the columns of letters formed by your message. Under the keyword, write the order of those letters when you alphabetize them. Now look at our example.

```
A P R I L
1 4 5 2 3
```

The letter A of April is the first letter of our alphabet, so the number 1 is below it. The letter I is the second one you find as you alphabetize—then L and so on.

Now, to create your secret message, write all of the message letters that are in the column under the number 1 (reading down, that's UIHD), then the letters under 2 (TITX) and so on. It will look like this—

UIHD TITX HPOJ SSEA ECRY

The person receiving the message first writes down the keyword (April). Then under each letter in April he or she puts its alphabetical number (A is number 1, I is 2, etc.). Finally, your private pen pal writes each group of words in its proper column. The first group, UIHD, goes under the first letter, "A." Since "I" is the second alphabetical letter to be found in "April," the second group, TITX, goes under the "I."

By reading from left to right, he or she will find the original message, "USE THIS CIPHER TODAY."

THE WONDERFUL WHEELIES

An Ancient Disk

This cipher machine was devised by a Greek in about 100 B.C. To make the wheel, have two photocopies made of the illustration on this page. (Maybe one of your folks can do this at his or her office, or you can go to your local library or photocopy place and they'll copy the illustration for a few cents.)

On one of the two copies, cut off the *outside* alphabet. Then, mount the small wheel onto the large wheel in the other copy. Use a thumbtack through the center and tack the two parts to a thick piece of cardboard or thin piece of wood.

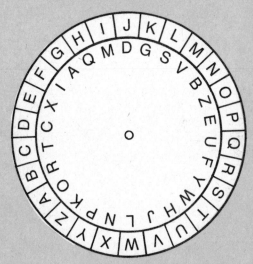

You use the wheel just as you used the Coded Shift in the section on Shifty Letters (p. 17). The advantage of this cipher is that the cipher alphabet (the inner circle) is all mixed up, so if a spy figures out *one* of the letters by accident, he or she still won't have the rest of the alphabet.

Here's how it works! Let's pretend that the message is "AT EIGHT SHARP."

You'd move your inner circle around a bit, and if the letter *inside* the A was, say, "O" write down an "O."

Then you'd simply write down the letter under each letter in your message.

So instead of the "A" in your message "At Eight Sharp," you'd put "O." Instead of the "T" (to complete the word "at") you'd write "W" (because that's what's under the "T" on the Wheelie). See? The "E" (of the "eight") is over the "X" of the inner circle, so you'd write "X."

To send the secret message "AT EIGHT SHARP," you would write OW XMAQX YQOFE.

The Flat Wheel

This cipher machine was invented by Thomas Jefferson for our army during the American Revolution.

Have five photocopies made of the drawing on page 25. Then cut each wheel so you end up with five different sized circles. (Cut one so it has just the inner circle of letters, the second, so it contains the two inner circles of letters, the next, three, and so on.) Put them together one on top of another. Use a thumbtack and mount them on a piece of cardboard or a wooden board.

To write your ciphertext (your secret scrambled message) set the wheels so that *one line of letters matches the first five letters of your message*. In the drawing the wheels are set for the message CIPHERS ARE FUN (the first five letters are CIPHE, and that's what the number 1 arrow points to).

Look around the wheels and write down *any one of the other 25 lines*. (Let's say the one at the second arrow is chosen. It reads RMOOF.)

Now set your wheels so that one line spells out the next group of five letters (the RS ARE of CIPHERS ARE FUN). Write down any *other* line of cipher letters you

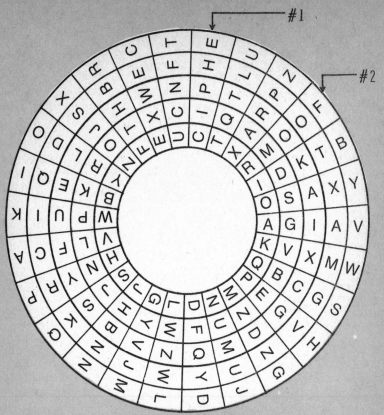

see around the wheels. (When the ciphertext for CIPHERS ARE FUN was finished, it read RMOOF ABCQF XJKZU. Yours will be entirely different, depending upon the message you want to send.)

When that mixed up ciphertext is received, your friend sets the wheels so that the first five letters (RMOOF) are in line. Then he or she looks around until another line makes some sense. These are sure to be letters of the message, so they get written down. Then the next five letters (in the example, they were ABCQF) are lined up.

Repeat this until you figure out the entire message.

PHONEYS!

If you came across this message, how would you go about figuring it out?

2/6/6/5.4/3.7/   27.3.   7.3.239/

If you know the key, it's very simple. Just look at the dial on a telephone. (In case your phone has pushbuttons, take a peek at the picture of the dial phone.)

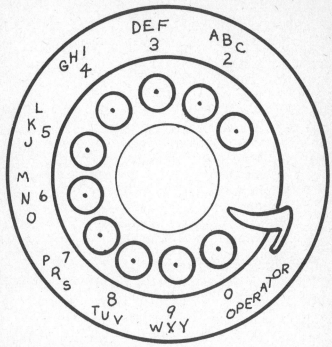

To decipher this hidden message, look for it on the dial.

There are three letters in each group around the dial, except at number zero, which will represent a "Z." If the letter needed in the message is the *first* letter of the three, then the sender would just put down the number of that group. If it's the *second* letter of the group that's needed, the number would have a period (.) after it. To show that the *third* letter is part of the message, a slash (/) is placed after it.

I'VE GOT YOUR NUMBER

Nothing makes a person feel dumber than to set up a system for sending secret messages—and then to forget the code!

Here's an easy code. Just use phone numbers as the basis for sending your hidden messages. You won't forget your own number, and you'll have your friends' numbers written down.

Here's how it works. Let's say your phone number is 527–1315. When you look at that number, you can see you have a lot of 1s. Think of each of the 1s either as being a 1 or as the first part of a two-digit number, like 12, 13, 14, etc.

The secret of this code is that you use your phone number (527–1315, remember?) as the hidden pattern—that is, the fifth word, the second word, and the seventh word would be the first three words of the message that you're trying to send, and so on.

All the rest of the words don't matter! The sentence you put together can make sense or not, as you wish.

So to send the secret message "The movie is at eight," you might create the sentence, "The movie I like the best is *Fantasia*, and I saw it at least eight times." And your friend would figure out your secret message this way:

5/	2/	7/	13/	15/
the	movie	is	at	eight

MESSAGE FROM OGAM

The Celts ruled great parts of Europe from 700 B.C. until about A.D. 100. They had a secret written language, which was actually a cipher. They called it Ogam. Since theirs was based on the Roman alphabet of 20 letters, it's been modernized for today's 26-letter alphabet.

Here is your key:

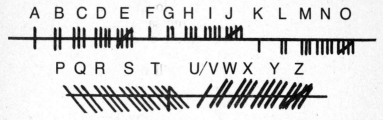

To write your cipher message, draw a horizontal (side to side) line across the paper. Now for each letter of your cleartext (the message) add the right little vertical (up and down) lines to your horizontal lines.

As you can see, some of the little lines are above, some below, and others across that long horizontal line. About half are straight up and down, and the rest lean forward or back.

Let's use the message "CIPHERS ARE FUNNY." This is how it would look in Ogam—

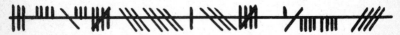

ASTRO CIPHER

These secret markings look like astrology symbols, so if anyone gets hold of one of your messages, you can always say, "Oh, that's just my horoscope!" Here is the key to the Astro Cipher:

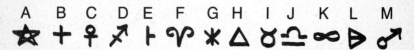

N O P Q R S T U V W X Y Z

◀ □ ♃ ☉ ∅ ≡ ♭ ▽ ☽ ♌ ♆ ♀ ♊

To make your secret message, draw a circle and divide it into fourths. The size of the circle depends on how long your message is. Start writing your ciphertext markings in the upper right section where 1 o'clock would be if you were looking at a watch.

Divide the letters of your message into four parts and then put the signs representing each fourth into one of the four parts, moving clockwise as you do so. If you decode our Astro Cipher, you'll find that it reads "IS JOHN THE SPY?"

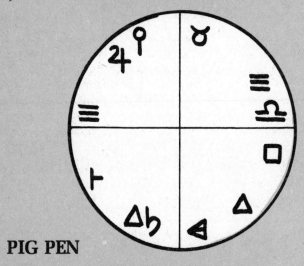

PIG PEN

If you want to keep a friend posted, here's a very pretty way to send a confidential message.

You'll notice that the alphabet is divided into two parts, and the letters are divided between the two designs. Each portion of the design contains and represents two letters. In other words, ⌐ represents both A and B. How do you know which letter to use? Simple. If your message needs the *second* letter, you put a dot in the center of the design. So, for B, it would be ⌐• . Got it?

Here's a quickie — a word for you to translate. The answer is below. It's upside down, so don't peek. First, solve the Pig Pen cipher.

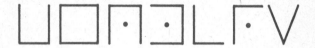

ANSWER: Ciphers

There's an even better way to cover your tracks. Buy a chisel-point felt-tip pen. When you make your Pig Pen designs, curve the corners and use thin vertical strokes, and it will look like you're writing Hebrew.

Here's an example of disguised Pig Pen writing.

ANSWER: Not Codes

THE SHADOW'S CLOCKS

The Shadow was a popular mystery story character created by Walter B. Gibson, who wrote under the name of Maxwell Grant. Being a professional magician, Mr. Gibson used many magical principles and unusual ideas in his stories, including a special cipher called "The Shadow's Clocks."

This is the key—

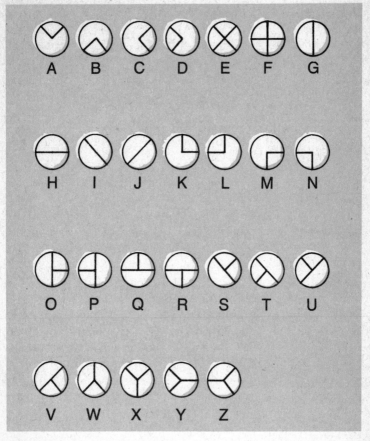

Trace or copy these symbols onto a sheet of paper, and read on.

There are four "change symbols" on page 32.

Every time you come to one of these "change symbols" in the ciphertext, you turn the paper on which the ciphertext is written *until the little line inside the change symbol circle points upwards.* This means that all of the symbols that follow will be turned in a different direction and will stand for different letters than before you turned the paper.

Here, try this sample and you'll see what I mean—

Cipher text:

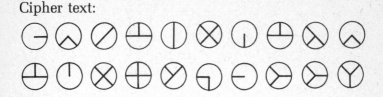

Change symbols:

Cleartext: C I P H E R S A R E F U N
               (CIPHERS ARE FUN)

GRAPHICALLY DIFFERENT

When you drop a line to a friend in this cipher, tell your pal to mix this paper in with some old arithmetic tests and no one will know the difference!

On graph paper, mark off a square with 26 boxes going across and 26 down. Think of each of the horizontal (side to side) boxes as a letter, from A to Z, and the same for the vertical boxes, A to Z, going down.

Let's suppose you want to send the message "MEET HIM TONIGHT." You write the cipher using the letters in pairs. The first pair is ME, so spell down to the M and then across to the E, and put a small circle in that square.

The next pair of letters is ET. Spell down to E, across to T, and put a small dot in that square.

Now draw a line from the little circle to this dot. Make a dot in the right square for the next pair of letters (down to the H, across to the I) and draw a line ET to HI. Continue on this way and your finished message will look like this—

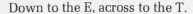
Down to the E, across to the T.

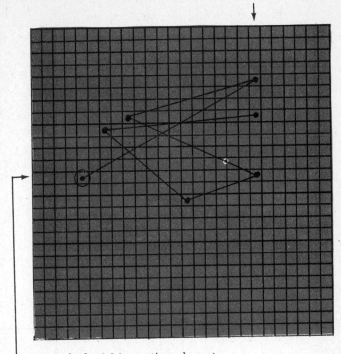

Start with the M (counting down)
and the E (counting across).

All your friend has to remember is that the small circle marks the first pair of letters.

STASH YOUR SECRET STUFF

Here is a great place for you to hide your most personal stuff — the keys to the symbols of your ciphers, the materials for your invisible inks, your cipher machines (like the Wonderful Wheelies), or whatever.

Take an old book that no one in the family wants anymore. It doesn't matter what the title is. Just make sure it isn't falling apart, and that no one wants it. Open it about 100 pages from the back and mark a rectangle in the center of the page.

33

Now hold the book so all those pages in the back of the book are exactly above one another. Don't let the right-hand edge be at a slant.

With a sharp modeling knife, cut along the lines of the shape you drew, cutting about three or four pages deep. Remove the papers you've cut out and trace that shape on the next page to be cut. Lift up all these pages with a hole in them, and cut out the shape on the next few pages. Keep doing this until you have cut through all the pages.

Put a dab of paste or glue on the outside corner of each cut page, except the top one. Close the book, put a couple of heavy books on top of it, and wait for the glue to dry.

You will now have a hollow book in which you can hide your secret stuff. If the opening isn't deep enough, then cut through some more pages toward the front.

3. Now You See It, Now You Don't: Invisible Writing

For hundreds of years, spies have sent messages written in invisible ink.

The most common ingredient for invisible ink is the juice of any of the citrus fruits (lemon, orange, grapefruit, lime). If you have one of these fruits in your house you can create a message that's here today and gone tomorrow!

You will need: citrus fruit juice (squeezed into a teaspoon), a wooden toothpick and a sheet of paper.

Dip the end of the toothpick into the juice and gently write the first letter of your message on the paper. Make sure you write without pressing down so you don't leave scratches on the paper. Dip the toothpick again and write the second letter. You'll need to dip your "pen" into the juice for each letter so that it will show clearly when it is "developed" later.

Then let the juice dry completely. To develop one of these invisible messages, all you have to do is expose the paper to heat. Holding it over a large lightbulb will usually make the writing appear. Another way is to have an adult iron the paper with the iron at a medium setting.

A good way to disguise the message is to write a regular letter in between the lines of your invisible message.

WET 'N WILD

Here is an invisible writing method that doesn't use *any* ink.

Dip the paper you want to use for your message in warm water. Lay the wet paper on a smooth surface (like a kitchen or bathroom counter or glass table top). Place a dry sheet of paper over the wet one.

With a ballpoint pen write your message.

Remove the dry top sheet of paper and throw it away. Let your wet bottom sheet dry out. The secret message will be invisible, but take my word for it—it will be there!

To "develop" one of these Wet 'n Wild message sheets, just dip the paper into water again. Now hold it up to a light. You will see the message you wrote, but it

will be in lines of *light*. This is a watermark, and it's done in the same way that manufacturers mark their stationery so that people will recognize their product.

By the way, when the paper dries, the message will once again disappear!

REFLECT ON THIS

This method for hiding a message works like magic.

Clean a little mirror (one in a compact is a good size) until it is beautifully clear.

Sharpen a piece of soap so it has a point like a pencil, and write a short message on the mirror. Make your letters a little larger than usual because they'll smear a bit.

Now rub the writing with a cotton ball until the letters disappear. *But as soon as the letters are gone, stop rubbing!*

Now the compact or mirror will look clean and will pass any kind of inspection. Keep it in your purse or pocket until you hand it to someone.

To develop the message, all your friend has to do is *breathe on the mirror*. What's left of the letters will stand out for reading, and afterwards he or she can clean off the evidence.

Do you think anyone will see through that?

Mally is telling Georgia a secret and no one can understand what she's saying. Read on and you'll find out how to talk in a tongue-twisting secret lingo, too!

4. Secret Lingoes

PIG LATIN

Pig Latin is probably the most common artificial language used in the United States. No one is sure how or where it started, but kids have been talking back and forth with these funny-sounding words for generations.

It's a simple language and uses just three rules.

1. When a word begins with a consonant, put the consonant at the end of the word, and add the sound of "ay," like in the word "play." For example, book = ook-bay; candy = andy-cay; me = ee-may.
2. If a word begins with two consonants that make a single sound ("th," "sh," etc.), move them both to the end, and then add the "ay" sound. For example, that = at-thay; should = ood-shay; speak = eek-spay. This is used for all words beginning with bl, br, ch, cl, cr, fl, fr, and so on.
3. If the word begins with a vowel, instead of adding the "ay" sound you use "way." For example, I = eye-way; on = on-way; are = are-way.

Ow-hay ast-fay an-cay ou-yay eak-spay ig-pay atin-lay?

As-way ast-fay as-way ou-yay an-cay!

LOCAL LINGOES

There are several tongue-twisting languages that are spoken by American kids only in certain areas, like on the East Coast or in the deep South. This means that if you and a friend travel to some other part of the United States on a vacation, you can probably speak one of these languages without anyone else knowing what you're talking about!

Almost all of these lingoes work by doing something funny with the first vowel found in each word.

"TURKEY IRISH" is spoken by using the following rule:

Add the sound of "ab" (like in "jab") *before* the first vowel. For example, cat = cab-at; dog = dab-og; candy = cab-andy; that = thab-at.

"POLISH COUNT" also uses the first vowel of each word. This time you add the sound of "op" (as in "stop") before the first vowel, and then pronounce the rest of the word. Here's how it works: desk = dop-esk; pencil = pop-encil; gum =gop-um.

Kids in Japan have a language all their own, too. They place the letter "k" after the first vowel, repeat the same vowel after the "k," and then pronounce the rest of the word. Here's an example of how that would work in English:

paper = pa+k+a+per = pay-kay-per;

note = no-kote.

CARNY

This slang is often used on the carnival lots or fair midways when a member of the troupe wants to say something so that it can't be understood by the "townies"—the people from the town where they're playing.

Once again you use the first vowel of each word, but

this time you add the two sounds of "ee-ess" before that vowel. For example, let's use the word "book." Start with the sound of "b," add "ee-ess," and then pronounce the rest of the word. It ends up "bee-ess-ook." Here are some other examples:

street = stree-ess-eet; wall = wee-ess-all;
store = stee-ess-or.

It's really confusing when you mix "Carny" with regular English, using Carny just for the important words. Suppose you wanted to say, "I'm going to see John's mother about going to the show." By mixing the two languages and leaving out a couple of unimportant words you have the following mind-boggling sounds:

"I'm going to Jee-ess-ons mee-ess-oms
about the she-ess-oh."

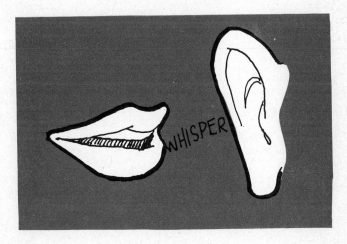

RHYMING COCKNEY

The same families lived in a certain part of London, England for generations. They were called Cockneys (although no one really knows why), and they developed their own special British accent as well as a private language. It's a very pretty speech to hear because its phrases are made up of words that rhyme. However, these phrases have no connection with the words they really mean. The Cockneys invented this language so outsiders — and the police — couldn't tell what they were saying.

In the 1800s many Cockneys got in trouble with the law. Because England needed people to be pioneers, some of these Cockneys were sent to Australia instead of to jail. That's why lots of Australians speak the slang too.

See if you can play with these Cockney phrases in conversations with your friends. (For example, instead of "boots," you'd say "daisy roots.")

candy—jack dandy

church—lean and lurch

cop—ginger pop

dance—kick and prance

drink—tumble down the sink

eyes—meat pies

feet—plates of meat

hands—German bands

home—top of Rome

jail—moan and wail

knees—bread and cheese

mouth—east and south

nose—these and those

pistol—lady from Bristol

shop—lolly pop

stairs—apples and pears

suit—whistle and flute

tea—Rosy Lee

NONSENSE NAMING

You and your gang get together and decide on new names for all of you. In other words, Doris will be known as Bunny, George will be known as Charlie, and Nancy will be known as Cathy. You'll notice we used names that end in "y" or "ie" as the code names. This is so they'll be easier to remember.

The next step is to use just initials for places and

objects that are frequently used by your group. The library is simply called "L," the 7-Eleven store is now known as "S-E," and bicycles become "Bs."

So, if you want to say "Nancy and I are going over to Doris's house on our bicycles for a private party," it would come out "Cathy and I are going to Bunny's H with our Bs for some I-C and Cs."

What are I-C and Cs? Oh, that's *ice cream and cookies!*

5. Signs of the Times

Most signs and signals are shortcuts.

Cattle brands signal which cow belongs to what ranch.

Mathematical signs are used every day, so we take them for granted. When you see a plus sign (+) or a minus sign (−) or the signals that mean divide (÷) or multiply (×), you don't even have to think twice. You know just what to do with the numbers in front of you.

Railroad signs instantly tell train engineers how fast they can go or what type of trouble they are about to run into. The sign at the end of the train (with the 60 in a diamond shape) means 60 miles an hour for the next two curves. In front of the train is a "W" sign that tells the man driving the train to use his whistle. And "NY-140" means that there are 140 miles to go to reach New York.

Now you're not likely to need to read cattle brands or railway signs, but there are some stationary signals around you that are fun to figure out and even more fun to do.

TRAIL BLAZING

The American Indians taught early settlers and hunters how to find their way through dense forests and over stony, bare sides of mountains. The Indians also showed them how to mark their trails so others could follow safely.

In these pictures of trail signs, you can see how the same signals were changed so they helped the settlers travel through the different types of countryside. Pioneers couldn't use twigs to mark the trail if they were in a treeless rocky area, so they had to point the way with whatever was handy!

The sign for danger is still used today as a signal for help, sometimes by shouting or knocking three times. It's a good one to remember!

This Way

Not This Way

Danger! Help!

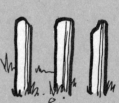

48

INTERNATIONAL
TRAFFIC SIGNS

After World War II the United Nations looked for easy ways for people to get around in any foreign country. It was most important that drivers of cars and trucks be able to understand this kind of information.

So instead of having a sign that says "school crossing" in any one of the many languages found around the world, they decided to use pictures on the signs. You don't have to speak the language of the land to understand the meaning of a picture!

We've started to use these signs in the United States, too. How many of these picture signs have you seen along the streets and highways in your part of our country?

Narrowing Road

 Men at Work

 Curves

 Traffic Light Ahead

 Rough Road

 Crossroads

 School Crossing

 Dangerous Crossroad

 Pedestrian Crossing

 Road Junction

 Falling Rocks

 Railroad Crossing

 No Entry

 No U Turn

 Road Closed

 No Passing

 Do Not Enter

 Quiet Zone

 No Turn in Direction Indicated

 Speed Limit

INTERNATIONAL MORSE

Samuel Morse invented a way of sending messages over telegraph wires using dots and dashes for letters.

Nowadays we no longer depend on wires for sending messages, but the International Morse Code is still used by radio operators throughout the world.

Here are the Morse Code dots and dashes for the alphabet, numbers and punctuation. You can use this code to tap or write messages to your friends. Since it takes a little effort to learn, you and your pals will probably be the only ones in your group who will know what's being said!

A	·—	D	—··
B	—···	E	·
C	—·—·	F	··—·

Letter	Code	Letter/Number	Code
G	— — ·	W	· — —
H	· · · ·	X	— · · —
I	· ·	Y	— · — —
J	· — — —	Z	— — · ·
K	— · —	1	· — — — —
L	· — · ·	2	· · — — —
M	— —	3	· · · — —
N	— ·	4	· · · · —
O	— — —	5	· · · · ·
P	· — — ·	6	— · · · ·
Q	— — · —	7	— — · · ·
R	· — ·	8	— — — · ·
S	· · ·	9	— — — — ·
T	—	0	— — — — —
U	· · —	Period	· · · · · ·
V	· · · —	Comma	· — · — · —

6. Silent Signals

You probably know lots of moving signals already.

ON THE FIELD AND COURT

Umpires and referees in many sports such as baseball, football, basketball, volleyball and soccer use arm positions to let you know what their decisions are, and to keep the game running smoothly.

In football, when the referee swings his arm in a full circle several times it means "time in," or "no more time-outs allowed."

TV STUDIO

TV stage managers wear earphones to hear what the directors tell them should be done. The microphone will pick up any sound in the TV studio, so the stage manager signals to the actors with hand signals.

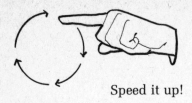

Speed it up!

The stage manager is signaling the half-minute sign.

AT THE AIRPORT

The next time you are in an airport or on a flight and
the plane is coming in for a landing, watch the men
who help the pilots drive the huge planes safely into
their "docks." They are called Landing Signal Officers
(LSO) and here's how they signal, using their arms and
what look like long flashlights:

This Way

Proceed to Next Signalman

Turn Left

Stop

Start Engines

Cut Engines

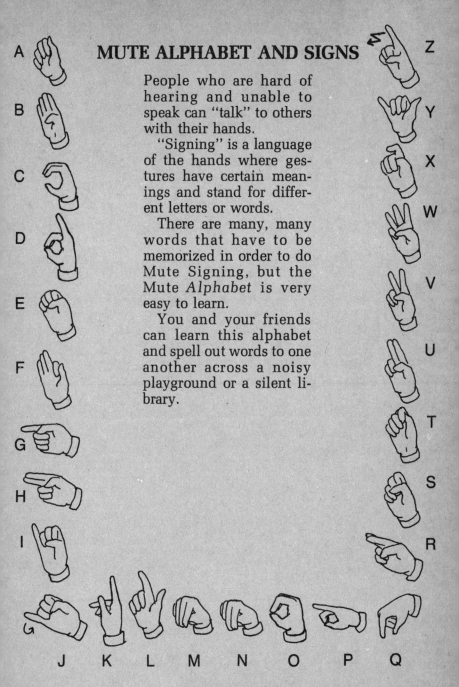

MUTE ALPHABET AND SIGNS

People who are hard of hearing and unable to speak can "talk" to others with their hands.

"Signing" is a language of the hands where gestures have certain meanings and stand for different letters or words.

There are many, many words that have to be memorized in order to do Mute Signing, but the Mute *Alphabet* is very easy to learn.

You and your friends can learn this alphabet and spell out words to one another across a noisy playground or a silent library.

7. Fingerprints: One Of A Kind!

Want to do some detective work? You've everything you need right at your fingertips.

Even if your hands are clean as can be, fingertips have oil on them, so you leave oil on everything you touch. Because you have lines on the ends of your fingers, what you leave behind is an oily pattern that is a different design from anyone else's in the whole world. That's your fingerprint!

Although no two fingerprints are alike, these designs are based on eight basic patterns. If you look at your own ten fingers, you may see as many as three patterns, and you'll surely see lots of differences from tip to tip. There are broken lines, dots and different widths in the lines that make up each pattern. Do you know that if you burn your fingertip badly enough for your body to have to grow a new skin on the finger, that the second skin will still have the very same marks as the original fingerprint?

If you want to see how different each one of your own fingertips is, slide the ends of your fingers lightly across the damp top of an inked stamp pad. Do one finger at a time, turning each one so that the ink is spread on all sides. Now roll your inky fingertips (one after another) onto a blank 3×5 file card. Label each finger of each hand and put your name in the center of the card.

Your pals' prints will look very different from yours!

It's fun to take a fingerprint off a smooth surface (a glass table top is the best). Press your finger down on the surface, or look for a spot where you think someone else's fingerprint may be. Now brush lightly with black powder. (You can make that powder by rubbing a lead pencil across sandpaper and dumping the powder into a small envelope.)

When the powder is on the surface with the fingerprint, use a soft feather or dry watercolor brush and very carefully brush off the loose grains.

Place a strip of clear cellophane tape over the fingerprint, press down, remove the tape, and stick it in the center of a blank 3×5 file card.

Now you can compare these "lifted prints" or your inked ones with the eight fingerprint patterns below, and you'll find out what kind of pattern you or the people you're fingerprinting leave behind on whatever is touched!

Plain Arch

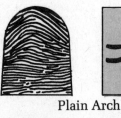

Ulnar Loop (Right Hand)

Double Loop   Accidental

Plain Whorl   Tented Arch

Central Pocket Loop   Radial Loop (Right Hand)

8. Tricky High Signs: Sharing the Secret

There are lots of really good mind reading tricks that can only be done if you and a friend know how to signal to one another without letting the audience know what's going on.

Here are five tricks. For most of them, you'll need a good friend as a partner. The two of you learn the tricks together. Then you can do them at parties or club meetings or in your classroom. For the last trick, you won't need a partner because you can get someone in the group to be your volunteer.

How can you and your partner signal to one another so it looks as though you're reading each other's minds? Simple. You use hush-hush communications!

A TEN-CARD LAYOUT TRICK

Here's What Happens

A deck of cards is shuffled. Ten cards are taken from the deck and placed face up on the floor or a table.

Your partner goes out of the room so that he or she can't see or hear what's happening. Someone points to any one of the cards.

Now your partner is called back into the room. You start pointing to and calling out the names of the cards on the floor, one after another. When you call out the chosen card, your partner says, *"That's the one that was picked!"*

Here's How You Do It

Place a ten — the ten of clubs, hearts, spades or diamonds — on top of the deck. Let's say it's a ten of clubs, okay? As you shuffle, mix up all the rest of the cards, but keep putting the top few cards back on top, so the ten of clubs never leaves the top.

As you deal out 10 cards from the top of the deck, that ten of clubs will be one of them.

Lay out the cards on the floor so they're in the same design as the little pips on the face of the ten of clubs, like this—

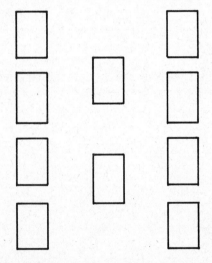

When your partner comes back into the room, you point to any card and name it. Your friend says "No, that's not it." You point to and name one or two other cards. Then you point to a certain spot on that ten of

clubs. The spot you point to is the pip which has the same position on the ten of clubs as the card picked earlier has in the layout on the floor or table. (For example, if the chosen card is the one in the upper right-hand corner of the layout, then point to the pip in the upper right-hand corner as you touch the ten of clubs.) Your partner says "Nope!"

Now you have secretly told your partner which card was chosen! You continue naming cards, and when you get around to pointing to that chosen one, your partner is able to say gleefully "That's the card that was picked!"

SHAPE UP!

Here's What Happens

Your partner leaves the room.

You show six pieces of cardboard, each cut into a different shape. There is a circle, cross, triangle, square, star, and hexagon (which has six sides).

Someone picks up one of the shapes, shows it to everyone and then mixes it up with all of the other shapes in a pile on the table.

Your partner is called back into the room. He or she picks up a pad and pencil, concentrates, and finally draws something on the pad.

You ask the person who picked the shape to find it and hold it up. Then your partner shows that the very same shape has been drawn on the pad!

Here's How You Do It

Use cardboard from the sides of cereal or soap boxes and cut out the six shapes.

If you look at these six shapes, you'll see that each one has a numbered quality about it: The circle has ONE outside edge. The cross is made with TWO lines.

The triangle has THREE sides. The square has FOUR sides. The star has FIVE points, and the hexagon has SIX sides. (You never call the audience's attention to these facts when you are performing, but you and your friend have memorized them.)

The two of you have also mentally divided the table top into six areas, as shown below.

Now you both know the secrets necessary to do the "Shape Up!" trick.

Place the six cutouts on the table top, but keep the pad in your hands for the moment. Ask your partner to leave the room. Then ask someone to choose a shape and pick it up. Put that shape back with the others and mix 'em all in a pile.

As you call your partner back into the room, *you casually drop your pad onto the part of the table which signals the number of the chosen shape.* (In the picture, the person picked the cross, so the pad was placed in the number 2 spot.)

As soon as your friend picks up the pad, he or she knows (from where it was placed) which shape is the

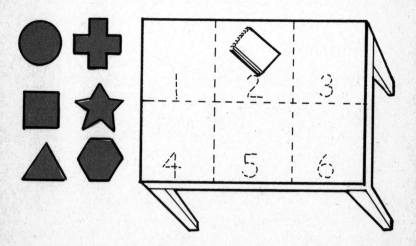

right one. But then your pal should pretend to think very hard before drawing that shape on the pad.

HIDING MONEY

Here's What Happens

While your partner is out of the room, someone takes a coin from his or her pocket and puts it on the table. You cover it with a cup so it can't be seen. Your friend comes back into the room, puts a finger on the bottom of the cup, and with eyes closed, names the value of the borrowed coin.

Here's How You Do It

There are only six coins that could have been used, and you and your friend have memorized this easy pattern: The 1¢ coin is at 1 o'clock, and the others are spaced in order—5¢, 10¢, 25¢, 50¢, and $1.00—around the circle.

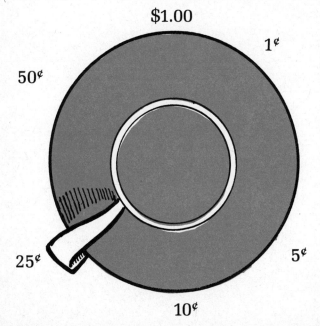

$1.00

1¢

50¢

5¢

25¢

10¢

When you put the cup upside down over the coin, you point its handle in the correct direction and your partner will know the correct value.

Make sure you both agree that the 1¢ position is always *facing you*. That way you'll both be using the pattern in the same direction.

WAD A MYSTERY

Here's What Happens

Your friend leaves the room. Now you ask each of the other people to think of a number from 1 through 9. Whichever number is called out first will be the one you write on a small pad.

Tear off the sheet; wad it up and drop it into a bowl. Ask everyone to remember that number.

Then you ask for more numbers, writing each one on a sheet, wadding it up and dropping it into the bowl, too. When you have six or seven, have someone mix up the papers in the bowl.

Call your partner back into the room. He or she reaches into the bowl, concentrates, then removes one paper. Opening it, your pal asks who thought of the first number, and then shows that the one picked out of the bowl is the first number that was called.

Here's How You Do It

When you begin the trick, you have a small bean hidden in your hand. After you've written the first number, secretly wad up the bean inside the paper, and drop the wad into the bowl.

Later, when reaching into the bowl to find the correct number, all your partner has to do is squeeze each paper until he or she finds the one with the hard bean in it, remove that one, open it (letting the bean slide secretly into the hand), and read off the number.

MIND-READING VOLUNTEER

Here's What Happens

You have the group decide who should be the Mind Reading Volunteer to help you with this test. You ask that person to come forward and sit with his or her back to the audience.

Now, three people in the audience each pick a card from a deck. They look at their cards and then put them back in the pack.

Handing the deck to the Volunteer, you say "Have you any idea which cards were picked?" Of course, the answer will be "No."

Then you ask the three people who chose cards to picture their cards in their minds as your Mind Reading Volunteer tries to find them in the deck.

And finally, your wonderful Volunteer holds up three cards, and they are the ones that were chosen!

Your secret signal turned an ordinary member of the audience into a part of the act.

Here's How You Do It

Earlier in the day, write this message on a blank sticker (or on a tiny piece of paper) and glue it to the *face* of one of the Jokers in the deck—

> Look through the deck and take out the 3 cards that are facing in the opposite direction from the others. Thank you for keeping this trick a secret!

Reverse this Joker (the one with the message on it) on the bottom of the deck so that it faces in toward the rest of the cards. Put the deck in its case, remembering which is the *real* top of the deck, and you're ready.

After your Volunteer is seated with his or her back to the audience, have first one, then a second, then a third card taken from the deck. Make sure no one sees the reversed Joker on the bottom of the pack.

As you go back to the first person to have the card returned to the deck, *you secretly turn the deck over.* (Because the Joker is face *in*, no one can tell that the deck is now upside down.)

When the three cards are slid into the deck, *they'll be facing in the opposite direction from the rest of the cards.*

Take the deck to your Mind Reader and as you drop it into that person's lap, flip the top card (the Joker) over on top of the deck so that he or she can read the message.

The rest of the trick is up to your Volunteer, and you will probably have a miracle!

HANDSHAKES

Lots of groups have secret handshakes so that when two members meet they can signal to one another that they belong to the same club.

Musicians often have special handshakes, which are quickly picked up by their fans as well. Here are handshakes that can be special signals for you and your friends or your club.

Jazzy and Bezazzy

You and your friend each put out your flat right hand as if you were going to shake in the regular way. Instead, you both touch the backs of your hands together.

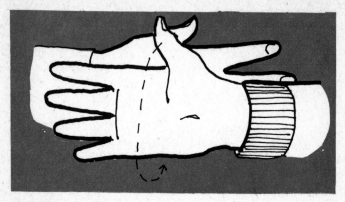

Now you both turn your wrists so the little fingers are still touching but the rest of the hands twist until both palms meet.

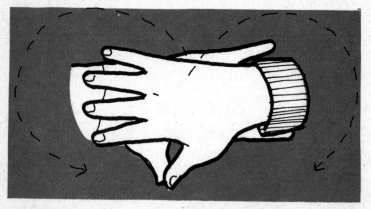

Bring the tips of your thumbs together. Keeping those thumbtips together, you each swing the rest of your hand toward your bodies and then swivel your hands outward, circling until the palms are touching again.

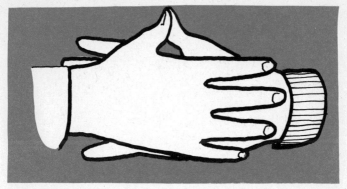

Now you slide your hand back toward yourself, saying "Make it," as you form it into a fist; saying "...shake it" as you wiggle it; saying, "...blow it" as you blow into your fist; then saying "...and stow it!" as you put your fist in your pocket.

Slapsies

You must know this one! When two people greet one another, one holds both hands out, palms up. The other one slaps both hands down on the upturned two palms and then turns his or her palms up so the slapping can be returned.

Knuckle Under

In this one, you shake hands in the regular way, but one of your knuckles is doubled into your palm. (Which finger you use will depend on which one you all agree on ahead of time.)

Link Your Pinky

Once again you start to shake hands in the regular way, but at the last second, you each separate your little fingers and link them together. Friendly, isn't it?

Wrist Lock

The wrist lock handshake is like the trademark of the United Nations committee promoting Brotherhood Week. You each grab your right wrist with your left hand and approach each other. Now your right hand grasps the other person's left wrist while his or her right hand circles your left wrist.

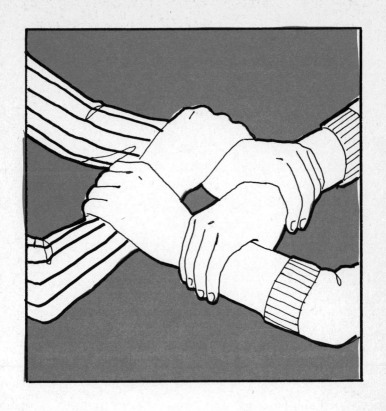

9. Garbled Games

SOME SUM!

A	B	C	D	E	F	G	H	I	J	K	L	M
1	2	3	4	5	6	7	8	9	10	11	12	13

N	O	P	Q	R	S	T	U	V	W	X	Y	Z
14	15	16	17	18	19	20	21	22	23	24	25	26

Here's an alphabet with a number below each letter. Your challenge is to write a list of ten 3-letter words that are worth a lot! When you've finished the list, add up the values of the letters. That's your score.

If you're playing the game by yourself, then make a second list and see if you can beat your first score.

For example, here is a list and its score—

BAT	2+1+20	23
COW	3+15+23	41
TRY	20+18+25	63
WET	23+5+20	48
SLY	19+12+25	56
TON	20+15+14	49
SAW	19+1+23	43
TAN	20+1+14	35
DOG	4+15+7	26
CAT	3+1+20	24
		408

SECRET SHIPMENT

You've intercepted a coded message about a shipment of animals and you've been able to decipher just this one word. Under each letter is the number used as the cipher for that letter.

C	H	I	M	P	A	N	Z	E	E
23	2	20	14	3	9	18	22	17	17

Below are ten more words on the list of animals, with the proper numbers under the letters. Can you figure out which other animals are in this shipment?

26	20	15	9	25	25	17		

3	12	8	2	4	18

14	1	21	17

23	9	14	17	21

8	20	26	17	15

21	21	9	14	9

21	20	4	18

7	9	26	1	9	15

26	4	15	20	21	21	9

17	21	17	3	2	9	18	8

3	4	15	23	1	3	20	18	17

77

DOCTOR, LAWYER, INDIAN CHIEF

This is the same puzzle as Secret Shipment except this one is all about what people do for a living. And the numbers are different, of course. If this job is:

A	S	T	R	O	N	A	U	T
8	5	21	18	9	1	8	15	21

what jobs are these?

| 20 | 9 | 4 | 21 | 9 | 18 | | | |

| 5 | 21 | 18 | 9 | 1 | 10 | 6 | 8 | 1 |

| 8 | 4 | 21 | 9 | 18 | | | | |

| 6 | 8 | 10 | 25 | 4 | 25 | 8 | 1 | |

| 21 | 14 | 8 | 4 | 2 | 14 | 18 | | |

| 5 | 21 | 15 | 20 | 14 | 1 | 21 | | |

| 6 | 8 | 11 | 9 | 18 | | | | |

| 10 | 8 | 18 | 20 | 1 | 14 | 18 | | |

| 8 | 4 | 21 | 18 | 14 | 5 | 5 | | |

| 1 | 15 | 18 | 5 | 14 | | | | |

CAMOUFLAGED CARTOONS

These top secret sketches are catchy clues. Each one represents some kind of a picture, but not what you might think. After you figure out what they are, draw them for your friends and see if they can guess them!

ANSWER: (reading from left to right, top row to bottom row): A bubblegum champ, germs avoiding a friend who caught an antibiotic, a soldier with a bayonet and his pet pig walking around a corner, a very close photograph of a camel passing a pyramid, a person playing a trombone in a telephone booth, tic-tac-toe game played by one person, two times four.

Here are two letters your spies have intercepted. Can you read them?

HIDDEN MEANINGS

The shapes of the words or the positions of words in relation to one another are clues to the answers.

For example:

> R
> ROAD
> A
> D

SAND	CYCLE CYCLE CYCLE
T O W N	111111 ANOTHER ANOTHER ANOTHER ANOTHER ANOTHER ANOTHER
STAND —————— I	
DICE DICE	

BUSINESS PLEASURE	l e
	     c
	c
	   r i
	A
	L
	L

WORM	
GROUND FEET FEET FEET FEET FEET FEET	MAN —————— BOARD
	ESGGESGG
	MEAL 1 MEAL 1

ANSWERS (reading top to bottom down the columns): Sandbox, downtown, I understand, a pair of dice, business before pleasure, the worm turns, six feet underground, tricycle, six of one and half-dozen of another, vicious circle, all in a line, man overboard, two scrambled eggs, one after every meal.

FOOLISH WORD PUZZLES

Each of the following puzzles is a famous saying about *Fools*, and is solved in a different way. They won't fool you if you look for clues. Don't fool around. Start now—


```
L E O G O N F A D E A R E         E
L                                 E R
S                                 R H
R                                 T
F U E S A H R I T N O W
```

DETRAPNOOSERAYENOMSIHDNALOOFA

THAW OFOLS SHEET STORMAL BE!

ANSWERS (from top to bottom): "Fools rush in where angels fear to tread." (Take every other letter and go backwards, starting at the top center.)
"A fool and his money are soon parted." (Spell it backwards.)
"What fools these mortals be!" (Unscramble each word.)

SECRET SILLIES

How many of the following messages can you read by pronouncing the letters?

A note hanging on a lawyer's door: I M 2 BZ 2 C U
An answer written across the bottom:
O U R, R U? I M BZ 2!

A verse: YY U R
YY U B
I C U R
YY 4 Me

A conversation: "ABCD goldfish?"
"UCNE goldfish?"
"SAR2 goldfish"
"OICD goldfish"

Written across a restaurant check: I O 0 4 I 8 0

I owe nothing for I ate nothing.

Oh, I see de goldfish!
Yes, 'ey are two goldfish.
You see any goldfish?
Abie, see de goldfish?

Too wise you are, Too wise you be, I see you are, Too wise for me.

Oh, you are, are you? I'm busy, too!

ANSWERS (reading from top to bottom): I am too busy to see you.

84

EARLY SHADOWS

This is a variation of The Shadow's Clocks, so it's called Early Shadows. Each of the following circles can mean either one of two letters, and you have to figure out which letter is needed.

Some letters are missing from the Early Shadows alphabet, so other letters that sound like the missing ones are used. (An "S" could be used instead of a "C.")

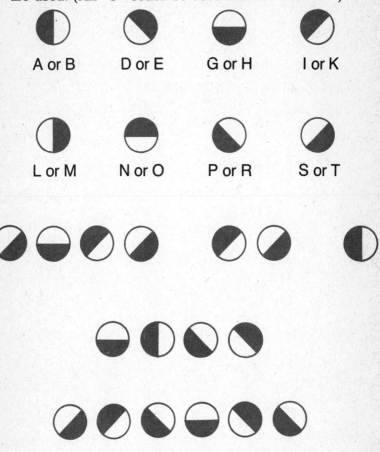

A or B   D or E   G or H   I or K

L or M   N or O   P or R   S or T

CIPHER CROSSWORD PUZZLE

After each of the definitions in the ACROSS and DOWN sections is the answer to that phrase. However, this answer is in cipher, and you'll have to work it out for yourself.

ACROSS

1. A small nail   ∨ ⌐ ⊔ ⊏
5. Deep, with water   93.5/5/
9. New name for Persia   ⊘ ⊖ ⊙ ⊙
10. To splice tape   3.34/8
11. Mountains in Wyoming   ⅂⊦⅊□◁≡
13. Carries   ※※ ₥ ※ ₩ ※
15. Not west   · · — · · · —
18. City train on supports   5–12
20. Purchasers   ⅃ ⟩ ∧ ∟ ⌐ ∨
22. Grocery sack   — · — · · — — — ·
23. K, L, …, …   ⊖ ⊙
24. Not on Ave.   ◐ ◐
25. He flew on wax wings   4/2/27.8.7/
27. Suffix meaning more   ⊦ ∅
28. Hindu teacher   ₋₋/ ※ /
29. French friend   · — — — · ·
30. Representative   19–25–13–2–15–12–9–3

DOWN

1. 10% for church   ∨ □ ∨ ⅃ ∟
2. Plural of "is"   · — · — · · ·
3. Not a dog   ⊘ ⊙ ⊗
4. String full of knobs   5.6.6/889/
5. Horse movies   ⊗ ⊦ ≡ ⅊ ⊦ ∅ ◁≡
6. MacMahon or Sullivan   ₩ ₩₩ —
7. Pot tops   ◑ ◐ ◑ ◐
8. Officer's rank   · — · · —
12. Negative   14–15
14. More than one of 18 Across   ∟ ⊡ ∨

16. Oriental adding machine 22.22/8.7/
17. Very sweet 
19. Fuming acid 6.4/87.4/2/
21. Large Australian bird 
24. Half 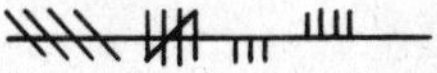
26. Sugar cane liquor ·—· ··— ——
29. Albert's nickname 

COMPUTER PUNCHLINES

Way back in the 15th century, a genius named Leonardo da Vinci studied everything around him. Once he had found out how something worked, he then tried to invent a way to make it better. During his studies he filled many notebooks, but for hundreds of years no one could read them. Why? Because he had simply written them backwards. That's usually called "mirror writing." You have to hold the writing in front of a mirror in order to read it.

Today you can do almost the same thing by using your electronic calculator. Certain numbers look like letters when they are upside down. Here are those numbers and the letters they resemble—

1	I
3	E
4	h
5	S
7	L
8	B
0	O

See if you can make the following stories add up to the proper words.

1. A man went fishing and had a very good day. He caught 15 trout, 150 bass, 95 halibut, 55 perch, and 2 old tires. Actually, his story was a _____ .

    $$15 + 150 + 95 + 55 + 2 =$$

2. Sixteen very cheap people, carrying a total of 42 pounds of baggage, went on a charter trip that cost a total of $79. But the Hawaiians heard they were coming and the whole group only got one _____ .

    $$16 + 42 + 79 =$$

3. A man told his workers to pick the 1,377 trees in each of his 4 orchards by the end of the week. They did it because he was _____ .

    $$1,377 \times 4 =$$

4. What is it that has 4 wings, flies 13 miles per hour, travels about 300 miles per day, has 6 legs, 3 eyes, and about 12 stripes?

    $$4 + 13 + 300 + 6 + 3 + 12 =$$

5. Five men took turns steering a boat for 101 miles each. At the end of that time a storm came up and they had to send out an _____ .

    $$5 \times 101 =$$

6. A farmer bought 10 acres of land at $710.50 each, because he liked the _____ .

    $$10 \times 710.50 =$$

Here are the answers in numbers.
To read the words, turn this page full of calculators upside down.

1.

4.

2.

5.

3.

6.

Index